YORK NOTES

The Merchant of Venice

William Shakespeare

Notes by Martin J. Walker

 York Press

The right of Martin J. Walker to be identified as Author of this Work has been
asserted by him in accordance with the Copyright, Designs and Patents Act 1988

YORK PRESS
322 Old Brompton Road, London SW5 9JH

Pearson Education Limited
Edinburgh Gate, Harlow,
Essex CM20 2JE, United Kingdom
Associated companies, branches and representatives throughout the world

First published 1997
Third impression 1999

ISBN 0–582–31449–6

Designed by Vicki Pacey, Trojan Horse
Illustrated by Clyde Pearson
Map by Martin Ursell
Chart by Kathy Baxendale
Phototypeset by Gem Graphics, Trenance, Mawgan Porth, Cornwall
Colour reproduction and film output by Spectrum Colour
Produced by Addison Wesley Longman China Limited, Hong Kong

CONTENTS

PREFACE

York Notes are designed to give you a broader perspective on works of literature studied at GCSE and equivalent levels. We have carried out extensive research into the needs of the modern literature student prior to publishing this new edition. Our research showed that no existing series fully met students' requirements. Rather than present a single authoritative approach, we have provided alternative viewpoints, empowering students to reach their own interpretations of the text. York Notes provide a close examination of the work and include biographical and historical background, summaries, glossaries, analyses of characters, themes, structure and language, cultural connections and literary terms.

If you look at the Contents page you will see the structure for the series. However, there's no need to read from the beginning to the end as you would with a novel, play, poem or short story. Use the Notes in the way that suits you. Our aim is to help you with your understanding of the work, not to dictate how you should learn.

York Notes are written by English teachers and examiners, with an expert knowledge of the subject. They show you how to succeed in coursework and examination assignments, guiding you through the text and offering practical advice. Questions and comments will extend, test and reinforce your knowledge. Attractive colour design and illustrations improve clarity and understanding, making these Notes easy to use and handy for quick reference.

York Notes are ideal for:
- Essay writing
- Exam preparation
- Class discussion

The author of these Notes is Martin J. Walker, an English teacher, examiner and journalist. He has worked on the GCSE English and English Literature examinations since the start of GCSE in 1988 and is now a senior examiner.

The text used in these Notes is the Cambridge School Shakespeare edition, edited by Jonathan Morris and Robert Smith (Cambridge University Press 1992).

Health Warning: This study guide will enhance your understanding, but should not replace the reading of the original text and/or study in class.

PART ONE

INTRODUCTION

HOW TO STUDY A PLAY

You have bought this book because you wanted to study a play on your own. This may supplement classwork.

- Drama is a special 'kind' of writing (the technical term is 'genre') because it needs a performance in the theatre to arrive at a full interpretation of its meaning. When reading a play you have to imagine how it should be performed; the words alone will not be sufficient. Think of gestures and movements.

- Drama is always about conflict of some sort (it may be below the surface). Identify the conflicts in the play and you will be close to identifying the large ideas or themes which bind all the parts together.

- Make careful notes on themes, characters, plot and any sub-plots of the play.

- Playwrights find non-realistic ways of allowing an audience to see into the minds and motives of their characters. The 'soliloquy', in which a character speaks directly to the audience, is one such device. Does the play you are studying have any such passages?

- Which characters do you like or dislike in the play? Why? Do your sympathies change as you see more of these characters?

- Think of the playwright writing the play. Why were these particular arrangements of events, these particular sets of characters and these particular speeches chosen?

Studying on your own requires self-discipline and a carefully thought-out work plan in order to be effective. Good luck.

William Shakespeare was born in Stratford-upon-Avon and baptised there in Holy Trinity Church on 26 April 1564. His family was quite wealthy, his father was a successful merchant and held several important offices in the town. Shakespeare was educated at the grammar school in Stratford, where he would have learned the common school subjects of the day: Latin, history, rhetoric and logic.

Shakespeare became rich and famous as an actor, producer and playwright.

He married Anne Hathaway of Shottery in 1582, when she was already pregnant with his child. William was eighteen when they married, Anne was twenty-six. They had a daughter, Susanna in May 1583 and twins, Hamnet and Judith, in 1585. It is thought that Shakespeare left Stratford around 1585, having possibly spent some time as a schoolmaster.

He is next heard of in London, where he met the Earl of Southampton, the man who was to become his patron (see Literary Terms). He is mentioned in records of 1592 as being an actor and dramatist in London. He is listed as an actor in the original performances of Ben Jonson's *Every Man in his Humour* in 1598 and *Sejanus* in 1603. After this time he probably concentrated on his own work.

By 1599 he was an important enough figure to feature in the establishment of a new theatre, the Globe, on the South Bank of the Thames. He wrote many plays for the Globe, and performed in them with his company, the King's Players. (An authentic replica of the Globe Theatre opened close to the original site in 1995.)

In 1597 he bought New Place, a large house in Stratford, and much land around the town. He retired to New Place in 1611, though he still visited London and maintained links with actors and theatre life. William Shakespeare died in Stratford on 23 April 1616 and was buried in Holy Trinity Church.

y

Shakespeare was a very successful and famous man in his own day. He was a favourite playwright of Queen Elizabeth and of her successor, James I. His careful cultivation of royal approval and his links with the Earl of Southampton gave him a privileged position. Shakespeare's plays were well liked by the public and he became very wealthy. It is difficult to think of a modern equivalent of Shakespeare, but famous film-makers such as Stephen Spielberg and Orson Welles are probably our closest equivalents. By today's standards, Shakespeare was a self-made millionaire, a difficult achievement in the twentieth century and a remarkable one for the sixteenth.

CONTEXT & SETTING

Why Venice?

In Shakespeare's time, Venice was the most important trading centre in the world. Goods from the Far East were traded in Venice and with them came new ideas and discoveries. The great explorer Marco Polo was Venetian and he had opened up trade routes with many new countries. To the English, living on an island and frequently cut off by war, the land we know as Italy held a great fascination. Italy was seen as a fashion centre and, largely because of its Roman history, as a centre of culture. Remember that at this time in England, only the wealthy had baths, and then perhaps only once a year, and that it was considered normal to be stitched into your clothes for the winter. Compared to England, Italy was a stylish and rather mysterious place.

The Jews in England

The explanation of Shakespeare's portrayal of Shylock is not a simple one. Today we think of different religions existing side by side as normal. This was not the case in Shakespeare's day. For one thing there were not really any Jews living in England at this time. They had all been taxed to the point of poverty and

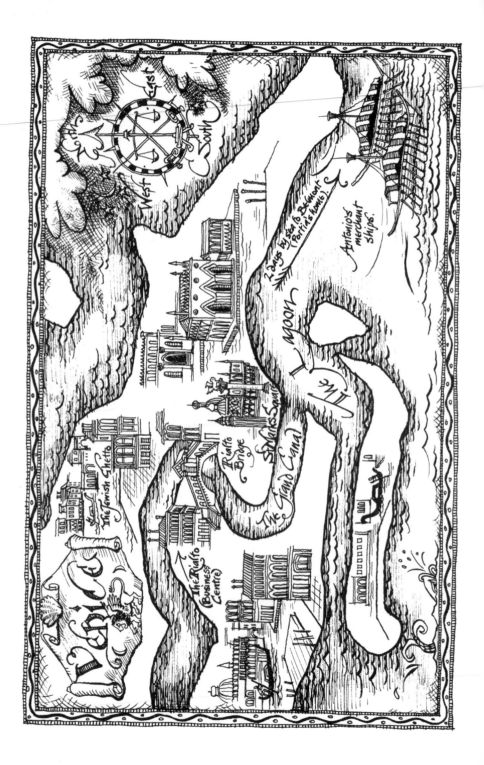

finally banished, three hundred years before
Shakespeare.

The idea of a Jew as used in *The Merchant of Venice* is
not based upon observations of real Jews. By the time
the play was written, only the old, medieval idea of a
Jew existed for people in England. The word *Jew* had
come to be applied to hard-hearted, unscrupulous
moneylenders, even though the people referred to were
not Jewish.

In 1594, not long before the play is thought to have
been written, the execution took place of the
Queen's physician, a Doctor Roderigo Lopez. Lopez
was a Jew who had converted to Christianity. He was
accused of treason after having fallen out with the
Earl of Essex and his death caused quite a stir.
Christopher Marlowe revived his play *The Jew of Malta*
in 1594-5 and it is possible that Shakespeare was
simply appealing to popular interest when he created
Shylock.

*Venice and
Belmont*

Venice is a city, whereas Belmont is Portia's house, set
some distance away. This idea compares well with the
fact that wealthy people had a home in London, which
they used when they had business at Court, and a
country estate. Women would often have remained in
the country when their husbands went to London and
this helps to account for the idea that Belmont is very
much run by a woman.

*Shakespeare's
use of sources*

Most of the plot elements of *The Merchant of Venice*
appear in stories translated from French and Italian.
As there are great similarities between Shakespeare's
story and some of these accounts, it seems highly
likely that Shakespeare had read, or at least heard of
them.

'Il Pecorone'
(1558) by Ser
Giovanni
Fiorentini

'Il Pecorone', which literally translated means 'blockhead', tells of a wealthy young man named Gianetto visiting the port of Belmont, in a ship supplied by his friend Ansaldo. There he meets a beautiful, rich widow about whom he hears that any man who can 'possess' her will win her wealth and her hand.

He enters into an unusual bargain with her: if he can spend the night with her and 'possess' her then he will be made lord and her wealth, lands and person will be his. If he fails to make love to her by morning then his ship and all its contents will become her property.

As Gianetto is about to retire to the lady's bedchamber for the night, one of the serving women gives him a drink. It is drugged and so, when morning comes, Gianetto has not claimed the lady, and returns to Venice without a penny.

Italian comedies
in the sixteenth
century were full
of life and wit.

He scrapes together enough money for another attempt but fails again for the same reason. To finance his third attempt to outwit the Widow of Belmont, Gianetto is obliged to borrow money from his friend Ansaldo. As Ansaldo's money is all invested in ventures abroad, he is forced, in turn, to borrow money from a Jewish moneylender. The story of the pound of flesh appears here exactly as it does in *The Merchant of Venice*. Ansaldo is duly bound to repay the sum borrowed by a certain date or else forfeit a pound of his flesh.

On his third attempt to win the Lady of Belmont, Gianetto has some help. The serving woman who gives him the drink warns him not to drink it. He stays awake, makes love to the lady and so impresses her by morning that she falls in love with him. He returns to Venice a rich man.

Y

The account of the lady dressing as a lawyer and outwitting the Jewish moneylender is also present in 'Il Pecorone', as is the business with the rings which occurs in Act V of *The Merchant of Venice*.

'The Orator'
(1596) by A.
Silvayn and
translated
from French
by Lazarus
Piot

This story deals in part with the tale of the pound of flesh and features a Jewish moneylender and a Christian merchant.

The four main elements of the plot of *The Merchant of Venice* were well known stories in 1598 when the play was entered in the Stationer's Register. Some were Italian stories of the sixteenth century whilst the episode of the caskets originated in medieval tales. Though Shakespeare borrowed from these various sources, he changed them sufficiently to suit his own dramatic purposes.

An Elizabethan audience would have been quite happy at the misfortunes of a Jew, a Spaniard and a Moor. Shakespeare was clearly giving the public what it wanted.

PART TWO

SUMMARIES

GENERAL SUMMARY

Act I

Antonio is the merchant of the title. His business relies upon buying silks and spices from distant lands and then selling them in Venice and throughout Europe. At the start of the play, all his money is invested in his ships, which are all still at sea. Bassanio, a close friend of Antonio, has fallen in love with the rich and beautiful Portia. He wants to visit Belmont, where Portia lives but dare not arrive empty handed. Bassanio has wasted his own fortune and a large sum of money loaned to him by Antonio. In spite of this, Antonio agrees to borrow money and give it to his friend.

In Belmont, Portia waits nervously as various suitors try to win her hand. She cannot choose her own husband, but must marry the first man to pass a test set by her late father. The test involves choosing the correct casket from caskets of gold, silver and lead.

Antonio and Bassanio go to Shylock, a Jewish moneylender, and a bitter enemy of Antonio. Shylock agrees to lend the sum of 3,000 ducats if Antonio is to be bound by law to pay it back. Instead of charging interest, Shylock says that he will take a pound of Antonio's flesh if the loan is not repaid within three months. Antonio thinks this is kindness, but Bassanio is wary of Shylock's intentions.

Act II

The Prince of Morocco arrives to take the test.

Jessica, Shylock's daughter, is planning to run away with her lover Lorenzo. He is a Christian whilst she is Jewish and so the two must act secretly. When she finally runs away, she steals gold and jewels from Shylock.

y

Morocco chooses the gold casket – the wrong choice.
Bassanio sets sail for Belmont as a second suitor, the
Prince of Arragon arrives there. Arragon chooses the
silver casket and also fails the test.

Act III   The news that one of Antonio's ships has been lost at
sea delights Shylock who begins to think that he might
now have his revenge upon Antonio for the terrible way
in which the merchant has treated him over the years.

Bassanio arrives in Belmont and, for the first time, we
see a suitor whom Portia would like to marry. She
desperately wants him to choose the correct casket, but
cannot give him any help. Bassanio selects the lead one
and in it finds a portrait of Portia, showing he has
chosen wisely. Bassanio's companion has, meanwhile,
fallen in love with, proposed to and been accepted by
Nerissa, Portia's maid. Before the couples can celebrate
their marriages, a letter arrives from Venice saying that
all Antonio's ships have been lost and that Shylock is
intent upon having his bond. The men leave for Venice
to try to pay Antonio's debt. They are wearing rings
given to them by their wives.

Shylock has Antonio arrested and taken to court. Portia
sends to her cousin, Doctor Bellario, for the costume of
a lawyer and a letter recommending her to the Duke of
Venice. She and Nerissa travel to Venice to help
Antonio. Lorenzo and Jessica remain in Belmont with
Lancelot.

Act IV   In court, no one is able to make Shylock change
his mind about the bond. Not even the Duke of
Venice can persuade him. Portia and Nerissa arrive,
disguised as a lawyer and his clerk. Portia plays along
with Shylock, saying that he is entitled to take a
pound of Antonio's flesh. She cleverly makes him
insist on following the absolute letter of the law.
As Shylock is about to take his knife to Antonio,
Portia says that he must not spill so much as one

drop of blood as blood is not mentioned in the bond.
Shylock has lost and is punished for attempted murder
by the confiscation of his wealth and by being forced to
convert to Christianity. He does not appear again.

Act V   Portia and Nerissa insist upon being given the rings
that Bassanio and Gratiano are wearing, as payment for
saving their friend.

Portia and Nerissa arrive back in Belmont just before
their husbands and pretend that they have never been
away. The wives ask to see that their husbands are still
wearing the rings they were given. Of course, Portia
and Nerissa actually have the rings. Bassanio and
Gratiano are humiliated in front of Antonio, who has
accompanied them, but all ends well when the wives
admit to their joke.

DETAILED SUMMARIES

ACT I

SCENE 1

In Venice, three friends – Antonio, Salario and Solanio
– are discussing their nervous feelings about one of
Antonio's merchant ventures.

The possibility of
losing everything
because of misfortune
at sea is clearly
shown here.

Antonio says that his gloom is not due to business
matters, upon which Solanio jokingly suggests that
perhaps the Merchant is in love. Lorenzo, Gratiano and
Bassanio arrive. Lorenzo senses that Antonio and
Bassanio wish to be alone, though the loquacious
Gratiano fails to take the hint. Lorenzo finally
persuades Gratiano to leave with him.

Bassanio would
rather talk about
money troubles
than about Portia.

Antonio and Bassanio now discuss the matter which
has been troubling Antonio. Antonio asks his friend to
tell him of the lady to whom he has sworn 'a secret
pilgrimage'. They talk about the rich and beautiful
Portia. Bassanio faces a problem in attempting to woo
Portia. She has attracted the interest of many wealthy
men and if Bassanio does not act quickly he could lose

Y

out. As her other suitors are rich, Bassanio feels that he cannot arrive at Belmont without money.

Antonio is quite prepared to lend his friend the necessary money but all of his fortune is invested at sea, and he does not have such funds readily to hand. He suggests that they try to find out whether such money is available in Venice and borrow it in his name.

COMMENT   We are introduced to Antonio's business. The idea of disaster at sea leaving a merchant penniless hints at future events.

In some editions   Salarino and Solanio are ambitious and want Antonio
Salarino is Salerio. to notice them. They are jealous of Bassanio and make sharp remarks on their exit.

Not only has Bassanio squandered his own fortune, he has also borrowed money from Antonio which he is unable to repay.

It is the foolishness Bassanio argues that if Antonio were prepared to loan
of Bassanio that   him yet more money again, he could use it to make his
leads to Antonio's fortune and repay both debts to Antonio. Bassanio
entrapment.   illustrates this, lines 139–51, with the idea of shooting an arrow in the same direction as one that has been lost and so finding both.

Bassanio mentions that Portia is rich before he says that she is beautiful. He seems as interested in her wealth, as in her.

Several of the references he uses to describe her are related to wealth, e.g. the Golden Fleece of the Jason and the Argonauts story.

Classical references such as this and the comparison of Portia to the wife of Brutus (Caesar's friend, assassin and 'the noblest Roman of them all') would have been understood by educated members of Shakespeare's audience and establish that Bassanio is himself an educated man.

GLOSSARY   **argosies** privately owned cargo ships
burghers citizens of high status
want-wit absentminded
alabaster stone often used for graveyard statues and tombstones

SCENE *2*

Nerissa seems to be Portia's confidante (see Literary Terms) as well as her servant.

In Belmont, Portia begins by complaining about her situation. She is quickly reminded by her servant and friend, Nerissa, that she is actually very fortunate and should concentrate on keeping a level head. Portia says that it is easy to give advice but much more difficult to follow it. Portia's father has stated in his will that Portia cannot choose her own husband, but instead she must marry whichever man chooses the correct of three caskets.

Nerissa then asks her mistress if she has affection for any of her suitors. Portia launches into a savagely witty attack upon the men who have presented themselves so far:

- The Neapolitan Prince talks only of his horse
- The County Palatine does nothing but frown
- The French Lord does everything to excess. Portia says that he would drive her mad
- Falconbridge, a young English baron, does not speak any of the languages that Portia speaks. He is good looking, but dressed in a mixture of styles from different countries
- The Scottish lord has done nothing but fight with the Englishman
- The German, the Duke of Saxony's nephew, is described as a drunkard

Portia dreads having to marry any one of these suitors.

*This links with
Bassanio's
intentions and
increases tension;
Bassanio must
arrive quickly.* Fortunately, these men did not like the terms of Portia's father's will and have recently left Belmont. Here, Nerissa reminds Portia of a young Venetian soldier who had visited Belmont in her father's time. Portia remembers his name instantly, though she tries to play down her interest in him. Portia is ready to say more about Bassanio, but is prevented from doing so by the news that the Prince of Morocco is on his way.

COMMENT Portia is not able to choose her own husband. This was quite usual for ladies at this time.

Arranged marriages were normal for wealthy people. Marriage was often carried out like a business transaction.

Portia is a very witty character as is shown by her remarks about her suitors.

Portia appears to be racist, attacking several national characteristics. In Elizabethan England, this would have been a perfectly acceptable way of creating humour.

The only man Portia has ever shown any interest in is Bassanio, hinting at later plot developments.

*Tension is
increased further
by the arrival of a
new suitor.* Portia's latest suitor is black. The Elizabethans found dark skin repulsive and a common insult was to say that someone was sunburnt. People applied white lead to their faces to be fashionable; many died of lead-poisoning.

GLOSSARY **surfeit** eat too much
Rhenish wine white German wine
Sibylla a lover of Apollo. He granted her as many years as she could hold grains of sand
complexion of a devil Morocco is black and Elizabethans believed that devils were black
shrive me than wive me hear my confession rather than marry me

SCENE 3

The first entrance of Shylock to whom Bassanio has gone to borrow money. Shylock is interested to hear that Antonio will be responsible for repaying the debt. He manages to hide his hatred for the Christians, and for Antonio in particular. Shylock is well informed about Antonio's business, and is fully aware that all the Merchant's money is invested at sea. The Jew reflects upon the disasters which might befall a ship at sea and then decides to take Antonio's bond. He then refuses to dine with the Christians and reveals some of his hatred for them.

Bassanio and Shylock speak in prose (see Literary Terms), but change to the more formal verse when Antonio enters.

Shylock tells the audience that he hates Antonio because he is a Christian. He plans to take revenge upon him for the ill treatment that he has received from the Christians. Shylock is often picked on because he lends money and charges interest; something the Christians are not allowed to do.

Antonio does not like doing business with the Jews. He is also very much against moneylending. He is forced to borrow money from Shylock and this angers him, especially when Shylock reminds him that Antonio has said that he would neither lend nor borrow money at interest.

Shylock justifies his business by telling a story from the Bible. Jacob was asked to look after his uncle Laban's sheep. He was told that he could keep any lambs which were born streaked or pied in colour. When the sheep were mating, he made a fence which was striped. The sheep saw this as they conceived and so the lambs were born with striped coats. Jacob was able to keep many more lambs than he might otherwise have done.

The 'devil' reference is both a common insult and an anti-Semitic one.

Antonio warns Bassanio that 'the devil' can recite the Bible in order to make himself appear holy. Antonio is quickly reminded by Shylock that he requires a favour from the Jew. Shylock then exploits the situation and recounts at length the ill treatment that he has received at the hands of Antonio. Antonio has

- Often insulted Shylock in public because of the Jew's occupation
- Called him 'misbeliever' because of his Jewish faith
- Spat upon Shylock's coat
- Spat in Shylock's face
- Kicked him as though he were a dog

Shylock asks whether a dog would be able to lend Antonio the money that he needs, and whether Antonio now expects him to be humble like a slave and give him the money.

Antonio despises the business of moneylending yet plays right into Shylock's hands.

Instead of remaining calm through this, Antonio loses his temper. The Merchant asks Shylock to lend the money 'not as to thy friends' but as if he were lending it to an enemy.

Shylock offers Antonio a deal which appears to come out of friendship. He says that he will forgive and forget the insults and the attacks made upon him. The deal is this:

- Antonio and Shylock are to go to a lawyer and sign a 'bond'
- Antonio will be legally bound by the bond

Antonio readily
believes Shylock,
showing he is not
so shrewd as he
thinks.
To remove a
pound of flesh
would mean
killing Antonio,
which is Shylock's
true purpose.

- The bond is in 'merry sport' only
- If Antonio cannot repay the bond by the due date, he will forfeit a pound of flesh

Bassanio is wary of Shylock's sudden kindness, but Antonio agrees to the Jew's terms without hesitation. Shylock says that he would have nothing to gain if the bond were forfeit as a pound of human flesh is worthless. Antonio is unconcerned about forfeiting the bond as his ships are due home 'a month before the day'.

COMMENT

Antonio's ability to repay the loan is dependent upon his ships returning home safely.

The conversations in Scene 1 about possible disasters at sea now become much more significant.

The balance of power shifts between Antonio and Shylock in this scene. Shylock manages to achieve the upper hand.

Christians could attack Jews openly, whereas the laws of Venice prohibited Jews from retaliating. Perhaps this is one reason why Shylock is better at controlling his temper than is Antonio.

GLOSSARY

ducats gold coins with the Duke's head on them
imputation suggestion
Rialto Venice's business centre where the stock exchange was
Nazarite Jesus of Nazareth
publican taxman
rated shouted at and insulted
gaberdine a cloak that Jews had to wear by law
void your rheum spit
doit a small sum, derived from the name of a Dutch coin

TEST YOURSELF (Act I)

A *Identify the speaker.*

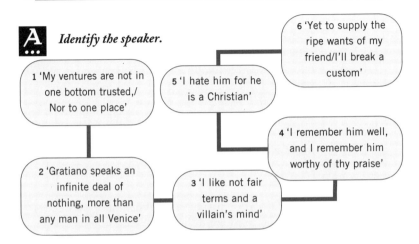

1 'My ventures are not in one bottom trusted,/ Nor to one place'

2 'Gratiano speaks an infinite deal of nothing, more than any man in all Venice'

3 'I like not fair terms and a villain's mind'

4 'I remember him well, and I remember him worthy of thy praise'

5 'I hate him for he is a Christian'

6 'Yet to supply the ripe wants of my friend/I'll break a custom'

Identify the person 'to whom' this comment refers.

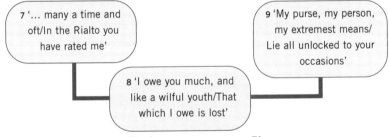

7 '... many a time and oft/In the Rialto you have rated me'

8 'I owe you much, and like a wilful youth/That which I owe is lost'

9 'My purse, my person, my extremest means/ Lie all unlocked to your occasions'

Check your answers on page 73.

B *Consider these issues.*

a The idea of shipwreck leading to bankruptcy for merchants is discussed in Scene 1. Look at how this has become even more important by the end of Scene 3.

b The way in which Bassanio sees Portia; not only as a wife, but as a source of wealth.

c It is important that Portia is seen to be a witty character. Look at how Shakespeare establishes this in Scene 2.

d Consider the idea of evil as applied to Antonio and Shylock, from what you learn about them in Act I.

e In Elizabethan England it would have been perfectly acceptable to be anti-Semitic. Bearing this in mind, Shakespeare still manages to make Shylock into a three-dimensional character and not simply a racial stereotype.

ACT II

SCENE 1

Portia's house, Belmont. The Prince of Morocco is the latest in the line of Portia's suitors, and intent on conveying his importance, his bravery and his wealth. Morocco challenges Portia to compare his blood to that of the fairest skinned person in the world to see whose is the reddest (red blood signified courage and virility). Skin colour was very important to the Elizabethans and this is one way of suggesting that Morocco is as noble as any white man.

The Prince is preparing to take the test of the caskets. Portia tells him that, if he fails, he must never ask any other woman to marry him. Morocco agrees to these harsh terms.

COMMENT

Throughout this exchange, Portia uses the word 'fair' to mean both attractive and white skinned. She does seem very concerned that she might end up marrying a coloured man.

Sometimes Morocco is played as a man with great dignity. There is ample scope in these lines for him to be played as a self important fool. Explore both possibilities and see which you favour.

GLOSSARY

nice rather fussy
Sophy The Shah of Persia
Hercules and Lichas a great mythical Greek hero and his servant

SCENE 2

Gobbo chooses the wrong word, a malapropism (see Literary Terms) intended to show stupidity

Venice, near Shylock's house. Lancelot Gobbo is on stage by himself and gives an account of how he decided to leave Shylock's service. There then follows an absurd conversation between Lancelot and his father, Old Gobbo, in which the old man fails to recognise his son. Bassanio enters and is immediately approached by Old Gobbo, who wants a new position

Y

for his son. Bassanio agrees to take on Lancelot as his servant.

Gratiano enters and tells Bassanio that he wishes to go with him to Belmont. Bassanio agrees on condition Gratiano does not misbehave and so spoil his chance of courting Portia.

COMMENT   This comic scene with Lancelot Gobbo occurs at the point where the audience want to see whether or not Morocco will choose the right casket. Comic scenes are often introduced to lighten the tone of the play and to keep the audience waiting.

Shakespeare often uses the notion of mistaken identity in his plays. Sometimes it results in tragedy; sometimes, as here, it is used for comic effect.

GLOSSARY   **devil incarnation** Lancelot means 'devil incarnate', i.e.: the devil made flesh
sand-blind partially blind
gravel-blind almost completely blind
ergo therefore
Gramercy God give you mercy
ostent appearance

SCENE 3   Venice; Shylock's house. This is the first appearance of Jessica, Shylock's daughter. She tells Lancelot that she is sorry that he is leaving. More significantly, Jessica says that she is ashamed to be her father's child.

COMMENT   This short scene establishes that Jessica is unhappy and gives her a clear reason to leave her father. She is, of course, already in love with Lorenzo.

Even though she is Jewish, Jessica says that she wants to leave her father's faith and become a Christian. This fits in with the general thinking of Shakespeare's time:

Jews were encouraged, even forced to give up their religion.

GLOSSARY **tears exhibit my tongue** Lancelot means 'inhibit', i.e. he cannot speak as he is so upset

SCENE 4 Venice. Gratiano, Lorenzo, Salarino and Solanio are preparing to attend a masque, and discussing arrangements when Lancelot enters, bearing a letter from Jessica. It appears to be a love letter addressed to Lorenzo, but after reading it, he announces that he does not need to look for a torchbearer for the evening, because Jessica is suggesting that she should disguise herself as his. Jessica is going to run away from her father and take some of his gold and jewels with her.

COMMENT In a Jewish family, the family line is passed on through the daughter, not the son as in most cultures. Shylock's daughter running away would have been one of the worst things that could have happened to him.

Jessica is prepared to steal from her own father. This would also cause him great pain, yet she seems quite ready to take his gold and jewels.

GLOSSARY **quaintly ordered** carefully organised
peruse this read this

SCENE 5 Shylock's house. Shylock tells Lancelot that he is free to go into Bassanio's service, and at the same time, calls for Jessica. Shylock waits impatiently for her. He has been invited to celebrate with the Christians and is uneasy about their reasons for inviting him. Shylock has had a dream about moneybags and he thinks that this is a bad omen. He is also concerned that his house will be attacked by the young men of the city as they make their way to the masque.

Lancelot tells Jessica to look out of her window as Lorenzo is on his way to collect her. Shylock goes, reluctantly, to the feast. Jessica tells the audience that she is about to disown her father.

COMMENT   Lancelot interrupts Shylock throughout the scene. His unwittingly comic remarks add to Shylock's growing frustration.

Shylock has not noticed his daughter's recent odd behaviour. He does not seem the most attentive father.

GLOSSARY   **rend apparel out** tear clothes by being too fat
wry-necked fife flute
patch idiot

SCENE 6   Venice, outside Shylock's house. The young men are on their way to the masque. Gratiano and Salarino are waiting for Lorenzo who is late. Gratiano says that people in love are usually far too early.

Jessica appears, on the balcony of her father's house, dressed as a page boy. She throws down to him a casket containing much of Shylock's wealth. Lorenzo and Jessica have planned to elope and they leave for the masque with the others.

Gratiano meets Antonio who brings word that the masque has been cancelled as the wind has changed direction and Bassanio can now set sail for Belmont.

COMMENT   Gratiano remarks that most things are better enjoyed when being chased than when you have them. Bear this in mind when he lands at Belmont. Bassanio gives up the expensive party very easily – he is a spendthrift.

GLOSSARY   **unbated** unrestrained

gentle a pun on the word gentile, meaning non-Jew

Cupid the god of love; Cupid was a blind archer

SCENE 7   Belmont. Portia shows the Prince of Morocco to the caskets and asks him to make his choice. Morocco reads the inscription on each of the three caskets. They are
- On the gold casket
  'Who chooseth me, shall gain what many men desire.'
- On the silver casket
  'Who chooseth me, shall get as much as he deserves.'
- On the lead casket
  'Who chooseth me, must give and hazard all he hath.'

Shakespeare deliberately delays Morocco's choice in order to develop the dramatic tension of the scene.

Portia tells him that one of the caskets contains her picture. If he chooses the right one then she will be his. Morocco takes a very long time to decide. He dismisses the lead casket as he thinks that lead is not worth hazarding all for, the silver casket, which does not appear grand enough to signify Portia, and eventually settles upon the gold because it is the most precious and promises to deliver 'what many men desire'. Morocco takes this to mean Portia. He looks at each of the caskets again before deciding. Finally, he chooses the gold, but the gold holds only a skull and, sticking out of one of the eye sockets, a scroll on which is written a nine-line poem, pointing out that Morocco has chosen foolishly. Portia is glad that he made the wrong choice.

COMMENT   The first line of the poem is often quoted. It is a warning that things are not always what they seem.

Morocco must now withdraw and is not allowed to propose marriage ever again.

A prince's word was not something that he could break. A man's reputation rested on his word.

Portia's final remark is a reference to Morocco's personality, but also to his skin colour. To a modern audience, Portia may well become a less sympathetic character because of her reaction to the idea of marrying a man with dark skin.

GLOSSARY   **Hyrcanian deserts** wilderness to the south of the Caspian Sea
cerecloth the shroud in which a body was wrapped
immured walled up
insculped inscribed
carrion death a skull

SCENE 8   Venice. Salarino and Solanio are discussing the
Look at the way   departure of Bassanio's ship. Shylock had attempted to
Solanio refers to   have the ship searched in order to find Lorenzo and
Shylock as a   Jessica. The ship had already sailed, but there have been
villain.   reports that Lorenzo and Jessica have been seen together in a gondola. Shylock is beside himself with a mixture of anger and grief. He does not seem to know whether it is the loss of his daughter or the loss of his money that upsets him most.

Clearly we are   News has reached Venice that a Venetian ship has run
meant to think that   aground in the English Channel. Solanio hopes that it
this might be one of   is not one of Antonio's ships.
Antonio's ships.
Salarino reports that, although Antonio is in debt to

Shylock, he has told Bassanio not to rush his wooing of Portia and so lessen his chances of success. Antonio has told his friend not to think of the bond made with the Jew. Salarino and Solanio set off to look for Antonio.

COMMENT Minor characters are often used to update the audience on recent events. This allows the plot to move along more swiftly.

Note the attitude of these two men towards Shylock. Clearly they see him as a figure of fun and are pleased that he has suffered, yet they would describe themselves as Christians.

Antonio is extremely kind to his friend. This contrasts sharply with his treatment of Shylock.

GLOSSARY **Narrow Seas** the English Channel
Slubber spoil because of laziness
stay the very riping of the time remain until you have achieved your goal
wondrous sensible having a strong effect upon the emotions

SCENE 9 Belmont, a room in Portia's house. The Prince of Arragon has arrived to take the test of the caskets. Portia shows him to them and explains the conditions attached. They are:
- He must never reveal to anyone the casket which he chose
- If he chooses wrongly, he may never ask a woman to marry him
- If he chooses wrongly, he must leave at once

Arragon does a great deal of deliberating as to which casket he will choose. He reasons that the message on the gold casket makes it too common for him to choose. He finally settles upon the silver one as he feels that he deserves Portia. (See notes on Act II Scene 7

This could be a jester's head, telling him he is a fool.

for an explanation of the message with each casket.) When he opens the casket he finds a portrait of a blinking idiot, and an accompanying rhyme telling him that he is a fool.

Arragon leaves, but before Nerissa can draw the curtain on the caskets a messenger arrives and says that another lord has arrived. The new arrival is Venetian and Portia is much more eager to meet him than she has been with any of her previous suitors.

COMMENT

Ar(r)agon was an ancient kingdom of north-east Spain. England and Spain were great rivals at the time the play was written. This helps to account for the portrayal of the Prince of Arragon as a fool.

It is possible that Portia knows which casket contains her portrait. Would this make her more, or less, nervous?

Portia obviously hopes that the latest visitor is Bassanio. Shakespeare does not reveal this yet, thus developing dramatic tension.

GLOSSARY

enjoined by oath bound by a promise

injunctions conditions

martlet house martin

to cozen to cheat

gleaned sorted out

iwis no doubt

wroth grief and annoyance

highday wit fine words of praise

TEST YOURSELF (Act II)

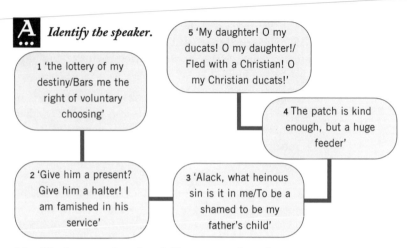

A *Identify the speaker.*

1 'the lottery of my destiny/Bars me the right of voluntary choosing'

2 'Give him a present? Give him a halter! I am famished in his service'

3 'Alack, what heinous sin is it in me/To be a shamed to be my father's child'

4 The patch is kind enough, but a huge feeder'

5 'My daughter! O my ducats! O my daughter!/ Fled with a Christian! O my Christian ducats!'

Identify the person 'to whom' this comment is made.

6 'For I am much ashamed of my exchange./But love is blind'

7 'Let all of his complexion choose me so'

8 'Bassanio, Lord Love, if thy will it be!'

Check your answers on page 73.

B *Consider these issues.*

a Portia seems to be a strong character, yet she allows herself to be governed by the will of her dead father. This gives us a clue as to the role of women in Elizabethan society.

b Shylock's own daughter disowns him and wishes to marry a Christian. Jessica can be a good character only if she converts to Christianity.

c Shylock is happy for Lancelot to join Bassanio's service as he eats too much.

d Lorenzo and Jessica use the language of typical lovers. The balcony scene is a little like that in *Romeo and Juliet*. It also suits the layout of Shakespeare's stage.

ACT III

SCENE 1

Venice, a public place. Salarino tells Solanio that the news in the Rialto is that Antonio has lost a ship, aground on the Goodwin Sands. Shylock enters and immediately confronts the two men. He is sure that they knew very well that his daughter was planning to run away. In the exchange that follows there is a good deal of word play, as outlined below:

Yet again, Shylock is referred to as the devil.

- Shylock accuses them of knowledge of his daughter's flight
- Salarino says he knew the tailor that made her wings
- Solanio says that Shylock should have known that a bird leaves its nest once its feathers have grown. He uses the word 'dam' meaning mother bird
- Shylock uses a pun (see Literary Terms) saying that Jessica is damned for it
- Salarino suggests again that Shylock is the devil

Shylock keeps referring to Jessica as his flesh and blood, but Salarino says that the difference between the blood of this father and daughter is like that between black and white. Shylock has heard the news of the loss of Antonio's ship. He calls Antonio a waster and then repeats three times that the merchant must 'look to his bond'. Shylock then delivers one of Shakespeare's most famous speeches. This is the gist of it.

This close repetition makes Shylock sound calculating and menacing.

- Shylock is intent upon revenge
- He recounts all the times that Antonio has insulted him and his friends
- Antonio did this simply because Shylock was a Jew
- A Jew is a man like any other. He feels the same things
- Christians exact revenge when they are wronged, so why shouldn't a Jew do the same?
- The Christian, Antonio, will be treated as he treats others

A servant brings a message that Antonio is looking for Salarino and Solanio. Tubal, a rich Jew, enters and Solanio comments again that the Jews can only be matched by the devil himself. Tubal and Shylock are left on stage and Tubal gives an account of Jessica's movements and action since running away.

Consider whether Tubal is gloating or truly sympathetic towards Antonio here?

Who do you think Leah was, if the ring means a great deal to Shylock?

Shylock's sadness at the loss of his daughter is mixed with despair at the loss of his wealth. He even says that he wishes Jessica were dead at his feet along with the jewels which she has stolen. Tubal tells Shylock that he has heard in Genoa, that Antonio has lost a ship near Tripoli in North Africa. Shylock is overjoyed at the news. Tubal also tells of the way in which Jessica has been spending her father's money carelessly: eighty ducats in one evening. Jessica has exchanged a ring which Shylock values greatly, for a monkey. Shylock vows to have the heart of Antonio if he breaks the terms of the bond.

COMMENT   Salarino and Solanio act as narrators, as they did in Act II Scene 8.

Much of the argument takes place in prose. This is unusual for major speeches such as Shylock's, lines 42-57.

Shylock's speech, lines 42–57 contains many ideas taken straight from the teachings of the Christian Church. He is using the Christians' own arguments against them.

The ring is of sentimental value to Shylock and, here, Jessica seems to have gone too far in her humiliation of her father, even though she may not have known of the ring's importance.

Shylock swears to take revenge upon Antonio for Jessica's behaviour, though Antonio is not actually responsible for this.

Y

GLOSSARY   **Goodwins** a dangerous sandbank in the Straits of Dover

slips of prolixity exaggerations

dam mother

Rhenish white wine

He was wont to he liked to

SCENE **3**   Belmont, Portia's house. Portia asks Bassanio to wait for a few days before making the choice of the caskets.

Portia says that she wishes she could tell Bassanio which casket to pick, but that she cannot. She is bound by the terms of her father's will. Portia realises that she has said too much, but adds that she is happy to talk as long as it puts off the moment when Bassanio might have to take the test.

Bassanio wishes to take the test immediately. He says that waiting is like being tortured upon the rack.

Portia tells Bassanio to take the test. She trusts that his love will lead him to choose the casket containing her picture. Portia compares her situation to that of Hesione, a beautiful young woman of Troy, who was to be sacrificed to a sea monster. Hercules rescued her and killed the monster. There is then some music whilst Bassanio examines the caskets.

The rack was an instrument of torture, used to make people confess to treason. Portia's recent experiences have made her wary of most people.

Think whether Portia really considers herself to be a victim?

In the first line of his speech, lines 73–107, Bassanio makes the comment that the outward appearance of something may well be the opposite of its contents. Bassanio says:

- Evil deeds are often explained away by citing a passage of scripture
- Cowards may grow beards to show that they are brave, but their livers are still white. (A white liver was thought to indicate cowardice)
- Beauty can be bought in the form of cosmetics, but the person who uses them the most is likely to be the least beautiful
- Curly, long, blond hair was considered beautiful, but many who appeared to have such hair were in fact wearing wigs made from the hair of corpses
- A beautiful scarf might hide dark skin. (The Elizabethans found dark skin unattractive)

Bassanio discounts the caskets of gold and silver and chooses the casket of lead. Portia is delighted at his decision and says that she can think of nothing else. She then tells him that she is really just an ordinary woman and not the fantastic creature he has just made *Note Portia's* her out to be. Portia says that everything she has, *change of attitude* including herself, now belongs to Bassanio. She gives *towards men and* him a ring as a token of her love. Gratiano announces *humble opinion of* that he and Nerissa have fallen in love and wish to be *herself.* married.

Lorenzo, Jessica, Salerio and a messenger from Venice enter. Bassanio is given a letter from Antonio which says that all the merchant's ventures have failed due to disaster at sea. Salerio says that Shylock is determined to have his pound of flesh; no one in Venice has been able to persuade him to change his mind. Portia offers to give Shylock much more money than he is owed and asks Bassanio to take it to Venice.

y

COMMENT   Portia is much less assured when speaking to Bassanio than to her previous suitors. She is nervous because she wants him to choose correctly and, more so, because she knows which casket he should choose.

Portia's speech, lines 40-62, ends in a rhyming couplet (see Literary Terms). This is unusual within a scene and tells us that something important is to happen.

Bassanio praises Portia rather too much. This could be due to his joy at winning her hand, yet also shows that he is trying too hard to be sincere.

We know Portia to be very strong-willed, yet she readily gives herself to Bassanio as if she were something he had just bought. She is a more conventional woman than she has made out.

GLOSSARY   **been forsworn** broken a promise

naughty wicked, a strong word to the Elizabethans

peize draw out

eche eke out

Swan-like end swans supposedly sang before their death

Of greatest port most important

twixt us twain between the two of us

SCENE 3   Venice, a street. Shylock instructs a jailer to imprison Antonio. The merchant tries to get Shylock to listen to him but the Jew is set upon revenge and will not listen to anyone. Antonio realises that Shylock wishes to kill him. He thinks, however, that this is because he has often released people from their debts to Shylock and makes no mention of his own appalling behaviour over the years.

COMMENT   As in Act III Scene 1, Shylock repeats a phrase about the bond. At this point, he is obsessive and beyond all reason.

Y

Not even the Duke of Venice can break the terms of the bond. Venice would lose its reputation as an honest trading centre if the Duke broke his own laws.

GLOSSARY   **gratis** for free, without charging interest
fond foolish
bootless pointless

SCENE 4   Belmont. Lorenzo praises Portia's generosity and tells her that she would be even prouder of her actions if she knew what a true gentleman Antonio was. Portia replies that she is sure Antonio must be very like Bassanio as the two are such close friends. She entrusts her house to Lorenzo and says that she and Nerissa will live in a monastery until the return of their husbands.

Portia sends her servant, Balthazar, to Padua with a note for her cousin Doctor Bellario. Balthazar is to take whatever documents and clothing he is given to Venice as quickly as he can. Portia tells Nerissa that they will both see their husbands before their husbands expect. The two women are to go to Venice dressed as men.

COMMENT   There is hardly any conversation between Portia and Jessica. This is in contrast to the sudden closeness formed between Portia and Bassanio and Nerissa and Gratiano.

Portia, lines 60–78, gives an amusing account of the typical behaviour of young men.

On two occasions, lines 61–62 and 79–80, Portia makes sexually explicit jokes to Nerissa. This shows her to be a little more worldly wise than she might at first seem.

GLOSSARY   **egal yoke** equal weight
traject the jetty used for boarding the ferry

S<small>CENE</small> 5

Note that Christians felt only they could go to Heaven.

Lancelot tells Jessica that he fears she is damned because she is the daughter of a Jew. She announces that her husband, Lorenzo, has made her a Christian. Lorenzo accuses Lancelot of having got a black girl pregnant. This is all dismissed as a joke. Lancelot plays upon words to the point that he becomes irritating. The lovers discuss Portia, and Lorenzo comments that he is as much to be admired as Portia is.

C<small>OMMENT</small>

This is an odd thing for Lorenzo to say. He seems to have a very high opinion of himself, though he may be simply making a joke.

This scene is another example of comedy being used to lighten the feel of the play. In practical terms it allows Portia to dress for the next scene.

G<small>LOSSARY</small>

got you not did not father you
Scylla In Greek legend a sea monster who dwelt on a rock of the same name
Charybdis a whirlpool
words are suited words are twisted

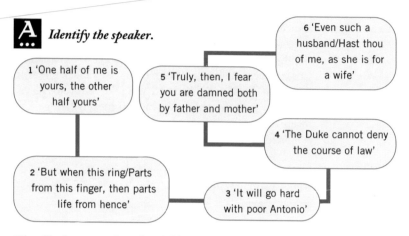

A *Identify the speaker.*

1 'One half of me is yours, the other half yours'

5 'Truly, then, I fear you are damned both by father and mother'

6 'Even such a husband/Hast thou of me, as she is for a wife'

4 'The Duke cannot deny the course of law'

2 'But when this ring/Parts from this finger, then parts life from hence'

3 'It will go hard with poor Antonio'

Identify the person 'to whom' this comment refers.

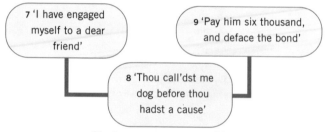

7 'I have engaged myself to a dear friend'

9 'Pay him six thousand, and deface the bond'

8 'Thou call'dst me dog before thou hadst a cause'

Check your answers on page 73.

B *Consider these issues.*

a Portia is very keen for Bassanio to choose the right casket, though she hardly knows him. Perhaps he simply seems like a good way out of her situation.

b Maybe Portia is merely pretending to be such a strong woman. She is very quick to pronounce that she is Bassanio's to command.

c In Act III Scene 2, Jessica has to listen to Salerio's attack upon her father, yet no one present actually speaks to her.

d Even when faced with a bad law which allows for persecution, the State of Venice is unwilling to consider a change in the law. This can easily lead to outrageous behaviour, such as that in Germany during Nazi rule.

ACT IV

SCENE 1 Venice the Duke's Palace. The Duke expresses his sympathy for Antonio, but Antonio says there is nothing more the Duke can do if Shylock remains determined. Shylock is summoned and the Duke pleads with him to show mercy.

Shylock stands by his promise to take the pound of flesh. He points out that if the Duke denies him his legal rights, the whole charter of the City of Venice will be worthless. Shylock refuses to explain himself and simply says that it pleases him to have a pound of Antonio's flesh. Despite Bassanio's attempts to reason with Shylock, he will not change his mind.

Antonio has resigned himself to his fate and is prepared to let Shylock have his way. Bassanio offers the Jew twice the money he is owed but Shylock says he would not accept even six times the debt.

Balthazar is the name of Portia's servant. She does not seem very imaginative.

Nerissa enters, disguised as a lawyer's clerk and gives the Duke a letter from the learned Doctor Bellario. Gratiano makes a vicious verbal attack upon Shylock but he still refuses to change his mind. Portia enters, disguised as Doctor Balthazar, and appeals to Shylock for mercy. Shylock insists on the law being upheld, even after Portia offers him three times the money. Portia says that Shylock is quite entitled under the law to cut off a pound of Antonio's flesh and Shylock thinks that the lawyer is as wise as Daniel. Portia asks for a surgeon to be brought to stop Antonio from bleeding to death but Shylock will not allow this as it is not stated in the terms of the bond. Antonio prepares to die and Bassanio says that even though he has just married, he would gladly give himself, his wife and all the world to save Antonio. Portia adds that his wife would not thank him for making such an offer and Gratiano announces that he wishes his wife were dead so that she could plead with God to make Shylock change his mind.

Portia is setting a trap for Shylock to do with the absolute letter of the law.

Shylock is about to cut into Antonio's flesh when Portia stops him. She points out that the bond allows him to take a pound of flesh, but does not mention shedding one drop of blood. Antonio is saved.

Portia springs that trap she has laid for Shylock.

Portia then pursues Shylock by insisting upon the following:

- Shylock shall have only his bond. He cannot now decide to take the money which he earlier refused
- By attempting to kill a Christian, Shylock has broken the laws of Venice
- Under these laws, the victim (Antonio) is due half of Shylock's wealth and the state of Venice the other half
- In addition, Shylock's life is in the hands of the Duke

Antonio gives his half of Shylock's goods to Lorenzo and Jessica as a wedding present. He then insists that Shylock convert to Christianity and make Lorenzo and Jessica beneficiaries of his will.

Think whether Antonio goes too far here, bearing in mind what Portia has already done.

Portia says she will take no money for her services, but insists that Bassanio should give her his ring, which he does. This troubles him greatly as he has promised never to part with it.

COMMENT Shylock is quite entitled to take a pound of flesh. He insists that he is acting lawfully but fails to see that the law is intended to be just.

The same Christians who think Shylock is unjust keep slaves. The law allows this and so they think it is acceptable.

Portia's speech about the quality of mercy is very famous. She shows here that she is intelligent and sensitive. It also balances the Duke's earlier (and more prosaic) plea for mercy.

The laws regarding an 'alien' plotting the murder of a citizen apply to Shylock because he is Jewish. A Christian would not receive such harsh treatment.

Portia is using the ring to test her husband. She may also be interested to see whether he puts his loyalty to Antonio before his loyalty to her.

GLOSSARY **Turks and Tartars** non-Christians who were despised, much as the Jews were

viands foods

inexecrable cursed beyond redemption

unhallowed dam unholy mother

Barabbas a Jewish thief who was said to have been crucified with Jesus

SCENE *2* A street in Venice. Portia sends Nerissa to find Shylock's house. Nerissa is to ask Shylock to sign a deed naming Lorenzo and Jessica as his heirs. Gratiano brings Bassanio's ring to Portia and Nerissa thinks it would be amusing to try to get Gratiano to *Note how Portia* part with the ring that she has given him. Portia says *is planning a test* that the two women will turn old listening to their *of loyalty for her* husbands swearing that they gave the rings away to *husband.* men.

COMMENT   Portia moves very quickly from pursuing Shylock to
arranging an elaborate practical joke. Clearly the fate of
Shylock does not trouble her concience in the slightest.

GLOSSARY   I warrant I swear
outface them stare them out, last longer than them in a battle
of wills

TEST YOURSELF (Act IV)

A Identify the speaker.

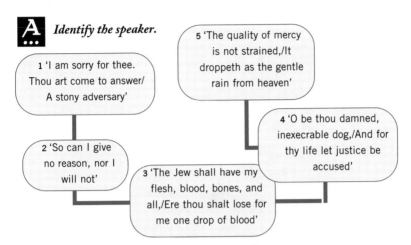

5 'The quality of mercy is not strained,/It droppeth as the gentle rain from heaven'

1 'I am sorry for thee. Thou art come to answer/ A stony adversary'

2 'So can I give no reason, nor I will not'

3 'The Jew shall have my flesh, blood, bones, and all,/Ere thou shalt lose for me one drop of blood'

4 'O be thou damned, inexecrable dog,/And for thy life let justice be accused'

Identify the person 'to whom' this comment refers.

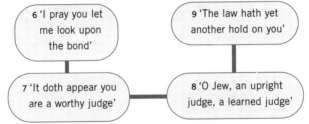

6 'I pray you let me look upon the bond'

9 'The law hath yet another hold on you'

7 'It doth appear you are a worthy judge'

8 'O Jew, an upright judge, a learned judge'

Check your answers on page 73.

B Consider these issues.

a Shylock tries to use the laws of Christians against them. He almost succeeds, but fails because he takes the laws literally.

b There is a warning here about obeying a bad law.

c Portia's intelligent actions in the trial give us hints about Shakespeare's view of women.

d Portia is thought of as honest and virtuous, yet she punishes Shylock severely.

e Portia is clearly annoyed at Bassanio's devotion to Antonio. Look at how she sets a trap for him in order to test his loyalty. The ring plot also ties in the final Act very neatly.

ACT V

Has Portia suddenly found religion, or is there another reason?

Belmont, Portia's garden. Lorenzo and Jessica are interrupted by the arrival of Stephano, bringing news that Portia will arrive home before dawn. She has been delayed as she has taken time to pray at several holy shrines. Lancelot stumbles around in the dark looking for Lorenzo, finds him and announces that Bassanio is also due home before daybreak. Lorenzo arranges for music to be played to welcome home Portia and Bassanio. Lorenzo links this to the belief that the stars in the heavens made music when they moved. He believes in the power of music to create atmosphere and feels that gentle music can calm the wildest beast.

Portia and Nerissa enter and are drawn into the romantic atmosphere created by the music. When the music stops the characters become much more straightforward in the way they talk. Portia finds out that Bassanio and Gratiano have not yet arrived and gives orders that no one should mention that the women have also been away.

Portia is clearly setting up the business about the missing rings.

The husbands arrive with Antonio. Bassanio immediately flatters Portia, saying that she is like the sun to him. She makes a sexually explicit joke, then remembers herself and greets Antonio. Nerissa has

Remember that, at this point, Portia has not yet slept with her husband.

challenged Gratiano as to why he is not wearing the ring she gave him, and accuses him of having given it to a woman — which, of course, he has. Portia joins in the telling off and, to make Gratiano feel worse, says that she gave a ring to Bassanio but that he would never have given his away. Gratiano swears that Bassanio gave his ring to the judge whilst he gave his to the clerk. Portia adds to her husband's discomfort by saying that she will never sleep with him until she has seen the ring and Nerissa promises the same to Gratiano. Bassanio begs Portia to believe that he has not given the ring to a woman; the joke is that he has.

The terms lawyer, doctor and judge are used to mean the same thing here.

The situation is taken one stage further when Portia insists that she will have the lawyer for her bedfellow. She cannot do anything else since she is, in fact, the lawyer. Nerissa makes a similar pronouncement and Antonio feels that he must intervene to support his friends. At this, Portia produces Bassanio's ring and says that she received it from the doctor after having slept with him. The men are amazed at their wives' behaviour. Portia finally lets them off the hook by giving them a letter from Doctor Bellario explaining that she had been the lawyer and Nerissa her clerk. She also gives Antonio a letter which tells him that three of his ships have arrived safely.

The couples retire to bed after further joking from Gratiano.

COMMENT

Lorenzo and Jessica speak like typical lovers. Note the repetition of the phrase 'In such a night'.

The stories told by Lorenzo and Jessica deal with tragedy and betrayal. This seems unusually gloomy for two newly weds.

The conversations between the two couples are full of

sexual innuendo. They almost forget themselves and embarrass their guests.

Portia and Nerissa continue the joke about the rings, but may go a little too far. Their treatment of their husbands is quite cruel.

Bassanio could lie about the loss of the ring, yet he chooses to tell Portia the truth. This is a little unexpected, as we have not seen this side of his character before.

Portia may have known all along that Antonio's ships had arrived safely. It is difficult to explain from where she suddenly produced the letter that she gives to Antonio. If she did know, then the whole trial scene was allowed to take place, purely for Portia's benefit.

Though three couples are involved in the play, Lorenzo and Jessica take little part in events once Portia arrives at Belmont. Portia does not seem to accept Jessica very readily.

The play is given a rather silly, happy ending in keeping with Shakespeare's intention for it to be a comedy. It is interesting to consider what Shylock might be doing at this point.

GLOSSARY

Troilus and **Cressid** Troilus was betrayed by his lover, Cressida

Dido Queen of Carthage, abandoned by her lover

Sola Lancelot is imitating a post horn

young-eyed cherubins angels in the form of children

Erebus a dark area of the underworld

Endymion a young shepherd and lover of the moon goddess Diana

cutler's poetry poorly written verse

prating talkative

mar the young clerk's pen castrate him

cuckolds men whose wives are unfaithful

inter'gatory question

TEST YOURSELF (Act V)

A Identify the speaker.

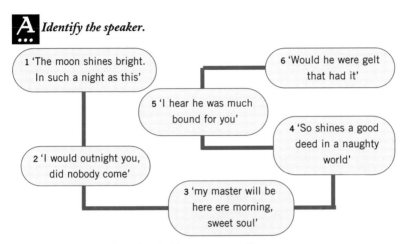

1 'The moon shines bright. In such a night as this'

6 'Would he were gelt that had it'

5 'I hear he was much bound for you'

4 'So shines a good deed in a naughty world'

2 'I would outnight you, did nobody come'

3 'my master will be here ere morning, sweet soul'

Identify the person 'to whom' this comment refers.

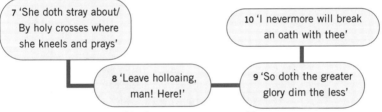

7 'She doth stray about/ By holy crosses where she kneels and prays'

10 'I nevermore will break an oath with thee'

8 'Leave holloaing, man! Here!'

9 'So doth the greater glory dim the less'

Check your answers on page 73.

B Consider these issues.

a Why Shakespeare chooses to have Lorenzo and Jessica discuss lovers who are famous for having betrayed one another.

b Whether or not Portia feels she has acted properly with regard to Shylock.

c How Portia feels about the arrival of Antonio on what is effectively her wedding night.

d Why Bassanio does not invent a story to explain the fact that he is not wearing the ring.

e How Antonio must feel when he sees his close friend Bassanio, for whom he had almost given his life, prepare to start a new life with Portia.

f How friends show their loyalty to one another in this Act.

Y

PART THREE

COMMENTARY

THEMES

There are several major themes in *The Merchant of Venice*. They could be described as:
- Bonds that exist between people
- True justice as opposed to the law
- The importance of marriage
- Revenge
- First appearances can be deceptive

All the themes are linked to the ways in which different people respond to the environments in which they live.

BONDS THAT EXIST BETWEEN PEOPLE

The bond of friendship

There are three clear examples of different types of bond in the play. From the very first scene in which Bassanio reveals that he is tied to Antonio through friendship and debt, and Antonio says that the bond of friendship between them cancels the debt, Shakespeare explores the bond between friends. This is tested when Shylock tries to take Antonio's life. Antonio's sacrifice for his friend is an example of altruism. He can be very generous to his friend and yet treat others badly. Bassanio offers to change places with Antonio so that his friend will not be harmed. The loyalty of friendship is further tested by Portia when she demands the ring from Bassanio. Because of the debt of loyalty that Bassanio owes her for the rescue of his friend, he has to break the promise that he made to his wife.

The bond of hatred

The bond of hatred between Shylock and Antonio is a central element of the play. It is this which leads to the actual bond of the pound of flesh being signed. Antonio and Shylock seem strangely bound together as they are unable to avoid one another. There is no

mention of other Christians hating Shylock as strongly
as Antonio does and Tubal does not report any such
problem.

Family bonds   The bond of family is the third type we meet. Jessica
decides that she is more strongly tied to Lorenzo than
to her own father. The play also raises questions here as
to whether she should have had to make this choice at
all. Lancelot and Gobbo are not close, even though they
are father and son. Portia's father's will shows his
concern to find her a husband who will not marry her
just for her wealth. Portia obeys her father's will though
there is little other than a promise keeping her to it.
These different strengths of family relationship are key
issues in *The Merchant of Venice*.

LAW VERSUS JUSTICE

The link between the law and justice is explored
thoroughly. It is clear from the behaviour of:

• Antonio towards Shylock

• Shylock when seeking revenge

• Portia when punishing Shylock

• Antonio when insisting Shylock convert to
   Christianity

• The Duke who lets events follow the law

that the law in Venice is not capable of providing
justice. Portia's famous speech asks for justice and
mercy, yet she does not show Shylock any such justice
when she insists on his punishment. The play questions
submission to a law which people know to be unjust.

QUESTIONING THE VOWS OF MARRIAGE

The strength of marriage vows is questioned through
the plots involving Portia and Bassanio, Nerissa and
Gratiano and Jessica and Lorenzo. At this time, many
wealthy people had their marriages arranged by their
parents. Portia's father has taken this one step further
by dictating the terms of his daughter's marriage from

beyond the grave. The vows of marriage are examined through the three couples and the following picture emerges:

- Two of the husbands break their vows at the first hurdle
- Lorenzo and Jessica are not fully accepted as a couple

Bassanio is tied to Antonio and there is the question of what Antonio will do now that his best friend is married. Jessica has betrayed her father and her religion and so is not portrayed as having the happy future she would have wished for.

In the play, friendship certainly seems to produce a stronger kind of loyalty than marriage.

REVENGE

Revenge occurs in various degrees throughout the play. The following are examples of revenge:

- Shylock attempts to kill Antonio
- Portia punishes Shylock
- Antonio makes Shylock convert
- Portia and Nerissa trick their husbands then watch them try to explain

The idea of appearances not being what they seem is another important theme of the play. Portia makes up her mind about her suitors after only having met them briefly. In the case of Morocco, she gives an opinion of him before she has even seen him. Paradoxically, Bassanio is very keen on appearances!

The two failed suitors, Morocco and Arragon made the mistake of choosing a casket based on outward appearances. The rhyme which Morocco finds in the casket is particularly appropriate to this theme.

The lovers seem to have made the decision to marry based on appearances. They cannot have known one another for long and the caskets serve as a warning to them that they might live to regret their decisions.

THE SEA   Finally, there is a background theme of life on the high
seas. The plot pivots on this: had Antonio's merchant
ships travelled safely, Shylock would not have been able
to demand revenge. The play abounds in sea imagery
(see Literary Terms), and an English audience would
have enjoyed all this familiar sea lore.

STRUCTURE

The play divides into several areas of plot and location.
The plots running through the play are:
- Antonio and Shylock: the pound of flesh
- Portia and the caskets: who will win Portia's hand?
- Lorenzo and Jessica: betrayal and elopement
- Portia and Bassanio/Nerissa and Gratiano: the rings
  used as a test of loyalty

These plots take place either in Venice or in Belmont.

Creating   In *The Merchant of Venice* Shakespeare creates moments
suspense   of great suspense. Much of the way he does this is
through his manner of switching between plots and
locations at vital points in the proceedings. Consider
the following examples of the audience being kept in
suspense:

In Act I, Scene 2 we learn that Portia must marry
whichever man chooses the right casket. At the end of
the scene the arrival of the Prince of Morocco is
announced, but we have to wait whilst Shylock and
Antonio agree the bond before we are taken back to
Portia. Even then, in Act II, Scene 1, we do not see
Morocco make his choice. We have to wait until Act
II, Scene 7 for this. By the time Morocco chooses the
gold casket, another plot has been introduced: the
planned elopement of Jessica with Lorenzo. Look at the
Table of Events on p. 52 and see how this develops
through Acts I and II:

Y

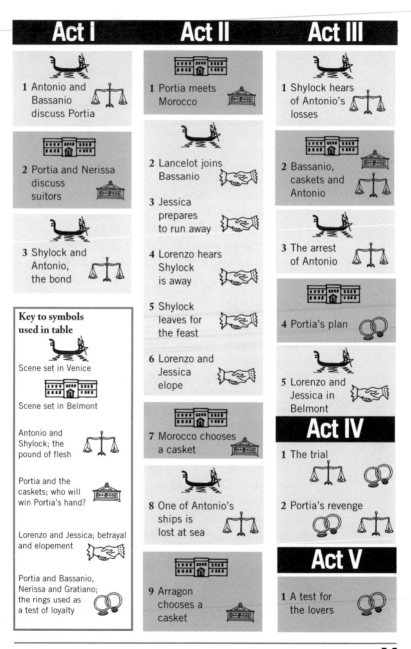

Act I

1 Antonio and Bassanio discuss Portia

2 Portia and Nerissa discuss suitors

3 Shylock and Antonio, the bond

Key to symbols used in table

Scene set in Venice

Scene set in Belmont

Antonio and Shylock; the pound of flesh

Portia and the caskets; who will win Portia's hand?

Lorenzo and Jessica; betrayal and elopement

Portia and Bassanio, Nerissa and Gratiano; the rings used as a test of loyalty

Act II

1 Portia meets Morocco

2 Lancelot joins Bassanio

3 Jessica prepares to run away

4 Lorenzo hears Shylock is away

5 Shylock leaves for the feast

6 Lorenzo and Jessica elope

7 Morocco chooses a casket

8 One of Antonio's ships is lost at sea

9 Arragon chooses a casket

Act III

1 Shylock hears of Antonio's losses

2 Bassanio, caskets and Antonio

3 The arrest of Antonio

4 Portia's plan

5 Lorenzo and Jessica in Belmont

Act IV

1 The trial

2 Portia's revenge

Act V

1 A test for the lovers

Shakespeare weaves the different plots together, never spending so much time on one that we forget about the others. Switching between plots in this way is used today in a good deal of television drama, particularly in soap operas.

Sometimes the audience is ahead of the characters, such as in the episode with the rings. On other occasions the audience is not shown something until the characters themselves see it, as in the choice of the caskets. By varying the use of these techniques, Shakespeare is able to develop both humour and dramatic tension.

CHARACTERS

ANTONIO

Antonio's position is high in the social order of Venice. He is not actually a member of the aristocracy and so can never have the power that the Duke exercises, but he is a wealthy and well known merchant, with all of the influence that money brings. The behaviour of Salarino and Solanio tells us that Antonio's friendship is a useful thing to have. A wealthy person who takes someone under his wing is known as a patron (see Literary Terms) and Antonio behaves as Bassanio's patron.

Though Antonio would have called himself a Christian, he has a vicious side to him. He knows that the law will support him if he persecutes the Jews and Antonio does not have the moral strength to resist acting like a bully. Just as many ordinary Germans allowed themselves to be swept along by the anti-Semitism of the Nazis, Antonio has been affected by the thinking of the time in which he lived. Shakespeare's audience would not have seen Antonio's actions as being unjust; they would have expected to see the Jew being punished.

Wealthy and well known

Loyal friend

Morally weak

Bully, hiding behind a bad law

At the end of the trial scene, it is Antonio who presses for the full punishment of Shylock. Considering that only moments before, his own life had been in danger, you might expect Antonio to show some mercy. He does not; instead he seeks revenge. Antonio's behaviour is really no better than Shylock's, but because Antonio is a Christian, the laws of Venice support him.

He is not a simple character. His appalling treatment of Shylock contrasts sharply with his strong loyalty to Bassanio. Antonio is, quite literally, prepared to die for his friend. The close relationship he has with Bassanio is often puzzling to a modern audience. Men would have spent a great deal of time together without any women being around and this has certainly been the case with Antonio and Bassanio. Antonio does not seem comfortable in the presence of Portia when they meet in Act V and there is no mention of Antonio wishing to find a wife.

PORTIA

Portia is a very strong character. Shakespeare often portrays women as being cleverer and more resourceful than men, and this play is no exception. Like all interesting characters however, Portia has a dark side. In Act I, Scene 2 she is first portrayed as a victim, helplessly bound by the will of her dead father. She then goes on to give a witty account of each of her most recent suitors, showing the Elizabethan bigoted attitude towards foreigners. When she first speaks of the Prince of Morocco, Portia talks of him having 'the complexion of a devil'.

Later, in Act II, Scene 7, she says : 'Let all of his complexion choose me so'.

Loyal to father
Very intelligent
Mischievous and witty
Capable of cruelty

This remark is clearly a reference to the colour of Morocco's skin, only here it is not made purely as a joke. She is no less racist than many of the men in the play.

Having seen Portia being strong, witty and racist, we then see her change completely once Bassanio has chosen the correct casket. She gives a very modest account of herself and immediately tells Bassanio that she is his to command as he is now her 'king'. This does not fit in with the sharp-tongued woman who gave such a harsh description of her suitors, unless she was simply 'acting tough' in order to put out of her mind the terrible prospect of marrying one of them. We might have expected Portia to keep Bassanio waiting, but she marries him at once. In some ways she is a far more conventional Elizabethan woman than she may seem.

The court is full of important men, yet it is a woman who sees the flaw in Shylock's thinking.

Portia's finest quality is her 'wit' (meaning intellect). She can argue better than any other character in the play, and it is difficult to imagine anyone getting the better of her. This is shown most clearly in the trial scene. Portia outwits Shylock and makes him talk himself out of having his bond by getting him to insist that it is followed to the letter. Her appeal for mercy is moving and extremely effective. After this speech the audience is very definitely on the side of the Christians and Shylock appears to be a wicked man. Once she has won Antonio his freedom, we see the other side of her nature in two ways:

The cruel side of Portia's nature emerges. Perhaps she is trying to be too much like a man.

- Portia insists upon Shylock's goods and lands being seized. She wants him to beg for his life to the Duke and delights in humiliating him
- Portia then behaves cruelly to Bassanio, her husband. She knows that it will be very hard for him to give up the ring she has given him, yet she insists upon it. She carries this on far past the point of a simple joke in some commentators' views

In Act V, Portia takes great delight in making her husband feel uncomfortable. Again, it might be said that she goes too far with this. She behaves like Shylock; she has tricked Bassanio into swearing to a bond that she knows he cannot keep and then torments him for breaking it. Portia seems very much in control of the marriage, despite her earlier statement that Bassanio was her lord.

It is also quite possible that Portia knew that Antonio's ships had not sunk, well before she went to the trial. Towards the end of Act V, she gives Antonio a letter containing the good news, yet she has herself only just returned. If she did have the letter before the trial, then it need not have taken place and was all for Portia's amusement.

SHYLOCK

Highly intelligent
True to his faith
Victim of racism
Bitter
Driven by hatred

The way in which Shylock is portrayed on stage has changed considerably since the play was first performed, when he was made out to be a villain and a clown. This changed in the nineteenth century when the actor Edmund Kean played Shylock as an intelligent man who had been victimised. Certainly Shakespeare did not write Shylock as a simple, one-dimensional part. He is one of the most complex characters in English literature.

To a modern audience, Shylock is sometimes a victim and sometimes a villain. The Elizabethans would have held the much simpler view that the Christians were always right and so Shylock was always in the wrong.

We first see him in Act I, Scene 3, when Bassanio and Antonio ask him for the loan of 3,000 ducats. Shylock is clearly plotting his revenge on Antonio, but our sympathy soon lies with the moneylender because of Antonio's bullying way with him.

Throughout Acts II and III, other characters add to this view that Shylock is victimised. Salarino and Solanio behave like Antonio, Lancelot leaves his service and even his own daughter deserts him. Apart from two brief episodes with Tubal, we never see Shylock with his own people, so we are usually given the Christians' view of him. The Christians invite him to dinner on the night that Jessica elopes with Lorenzo, and so betray his trust further. Against all this is the fact that Shylock pursues his revenge upon Antonio. The lines 'I'll plague him, I'll torture him. I am glad of it.' (III.1.91–2) show how bitter Shylock has become, yet we cannot help but feel that this is not all his fault. After years of being kicked and spat upon by men like Antonio, Shylock's hatred is understandable.

In the trial scene, he has the chance to show that he is far superior to the Christians. If Shylock were to show mercy to Antonio, then he would come out of the proceedings very well indeed. He does not show mercy, but presses on ruthlessly with his attempt to kill Antonio. When he is defeated by Portia, the audience is no longer on his side. If the play finished here, we would leave the theatre feeling that Shylock had probably got what he deserved. As it is, the harsh punishments he receives, first from Portia and then from Antonio, tends to shift sympathy back to Shylock. Perhaps the oddest thing about the end of the play is that Shylock does not feature in it at all. In the final part of the courtroom scene Shylock hardly speaks.

BASSANIO   Bassanio is a headstrong young man. At the start of the play he says that he has wasted all his own fortune and a sum of money loaned to him by Antonio. He is a little too ready to fall in love with Portia and, at one stage, seems more interested in her money than in her. He is quite a shrewd character as he sees the danger of Antonio signing the bond. He is, however, still prepared to let his friend go ahead and make the promise to Shylock.

In the presence of Portia he changes his behaviour. His is no match for her wit and he becomes a little too keen too quickly. This nervousness shows his lack of

*True and loyal
friend*

Playboy

Honest

experience with women. His long speeches before choosing the casket are comic as they are far too intense. He talks too much when excited and forgets to control his emotions in public.

He does prove to be a loyal friend to Antonio as he leaves his wife on their wedding day to travel to Venice and help him. He offers to exchange his life for Antonio's, at one point in the trial scene. Bassanio is rather naïve as he thinks that he can simply talk Shylock out of taking the pound of flesh. He does not seem to realise the strength of the moneylender's feelings and so misjudges the situation. He has trouble keeping his temper, calling Shylock a 'cruel devil' yet expecting to win him over.

Bassanio shows that he is an honest man during the business with the rings. It really troubles him that he has to give his ring to the lawyer and yet he does it as he feels it is the right thing to do. When Portia presses him for an explanation as to why he is not wearing the ring, Bassanio tells the truth. He could have made up a story or have simply said that he had lost it; instead he owns up to having given it away to the first person who asked for it. Again he is not very good at hiding his feelings. He is a much simpler person than Portia and her comments about Bassanio being her lord seem out of place when we see the two together.

G RATIANO   Gratiano is looked upon by his friends as being a clown. He talks far too much and not always at the appropriate time. Bassanio has been in trouble before now because of Gratiano's behaviour and is sometimes embarrassed by him. He cannot resist the temptation to make a joke whenever possible and loves the sound of his own voice. Gratiano thinks that he, himself, is very funny.

He falls in love with Nerissa in the time it takes Bassanio to choose the casket. This rash behaviour is typical of him. He also makes a promise about the ring without thinking of the consequences.

During the courtroom scene he does not help the situation with his strong attacks upon Shylock. Many of the characters present at the trial think the same as Gratiano, but he is the one who comes out and says that Shylock is an 'inexecrable dog'. He is easily outwitted by Nerissa and becomes very frustrated with her when she does not believe his explanation.

NERISSA   Nerissa is Portia's maid, companion, and confidante (see Literary Terms). She seems to have modelled herself on Portia and generally follows what her mistress does. She can be quite crude, though she is never as sharp as Portia when making jokes. She is prepared to put Portia in her place when she starts to complain about the life she leads and so has some independence.

LANCELOT   Lancelot is a comic character who represents the ordinary citizens of Venice. He is not interested in the important dealings of Antonio and Bassanio unless they affect him. He is preoccupied with getting himself a good position in life and happily trades one master off against another. He does reveal that he is also subject to the same feelings as the Christians. He makes several unkind remarks about Shylock. Lancelot is devoted to Jessica and has formed a genuine friendship with her, though he is not very sensitive in the comments he makes about her father.

Clownish
Funny

He serves to lighten the atmosphere of the play and his appearances tend to follow very dramatic moments. He also gives the other characters, such as Lorenzo, someone to make fun of.

y

SALARINO AND SOLANIO

The two men are quite wealthy citizens, though they are clearly looking for an opportunity to better themselves. They see Antonio as a good contact and are rather jealous of the attention that he shows to Bassanio. They act as narrators, filling in information on events that would have taken too long to portray on stage. They also reinforce the strongly anti-Semitic atmosphere of Venice; their comments about Shylock are as unpleasant as anyone's.

THE DUKE

As ruler of the State of Venice, he is the most powerful and wealthy man in the city and has the final say in major disputes. He appears to be fair, as he does not want to see Antonio killed, but equally, he does not break the laws of Venice simply to defeat Shylock. This might make him a poor ruler as he is not prepared to sacrifice his own reputation in order to see that justice prevails.

JESSICA

The daughter of Shylock and so, Jewish herself, she renounces her beliefs and disowns her father in order to be with the man she loves. She is quite cruel in the way that she leaves and unfair when she steals from Shylock. In fact the way she behaves towards Shylock makes a modern audience feel sympathetic towards him. Like the other lovers, she has made a decision quickly and the suggestion is that she might live to regret this. In the scenes at Belmont, Jessica is largely ignored by the other characters, especially Portia. Her conversation with Lorenzo at the beginning of Act V features stories of lovers who have betrayed one another and this points to possible difficulties ahead for this couple. Even though Jessica converts to Christianity, she may well not be properly accepted by the likes of Portia and Antonio.

Torn between romantic and family love

LORENZO

He has failed to consider how a Christian with a Jewish wife will be received.

A Christian and an associate of Bassanio, he has fallen in love with Jessica, though it is unlikely that the two of them could have met frequently as they come from different cultures. He takes her away from Venice without really having anywhere to take her to. They roam Italy spending huge sums of money unwisely and then arrive in Belmont and stay in the house of someone neither of them know. This shows that Lorenzo has not planned his future with Jessica. Perhaps the conversation about doomed lovers is more relevant than he thinks.

GOBBO

Old Gobbo, father of Lancelot, is nearly blind and easily confused. He fails at first to recognise his own son, but tries to help Lancelot to obtain a position with Bassanio. He often chooses the wrong word for the occasion, with comic effect.

THE PRINCES OF MOROCCO AND ARRAGON

A proud man who feels that he has as much right to marry Portia as anyone, Morocco is pompous and full of himself but proves to be honourable. Morocco can be played as a fool or as an important man who suffers discrimination at the hands of Portia.

Arragon is long-winded and full of his own importance. It should be remembered that Ar(r)agon was a Spanish kingdom and that the English and the Spanish had been bitter enemies for many years. The Prince of Arragon is an Englishman's idea of a Spaniard.

LANGUAGE & STYLE

There are two different types of speech used in the play
• blank verse (see Literary Terms)
• prose (see Literary Terms)
Most of the characters speak in blank verse. This is different from the way we normally speak. Verse has a rhythm, meaning that all the lines follow the same pattern.

Here is a line of verse from the play: 'You know me well, and herein spend but time'.

The line has ten beats to it, in its arrangement of stressed and unstressed syllables. The line which follows it also has ten beats to it: 'To wind about my love with circumstance'.

Verse is a convention that would have been recognised by the audience.

These are examples of blank verse. It is called 'blank' because it does not rhyme. This type of speech is used in two situations:

• Formal speech between important characters
• When something important is being said

Occasionally, a character speaks in rhyme. This is to let the audience know either that something important is being said or that a scene is about to end.

When we speak in everyday situations we do not speak in blank verse. Imagine how difficult it would be if everything we said had to be fitted into a pattern like the one above. What we would think of as *normal speech* is called prose.

The way in which a character uses language helps the audience to decide what sort of person he/she is. Here are some examples of different uses of language:

Verse is much easier to learn than prose

• When Antonio is depressed he speaks very formally and seems unable to relax.
• Bassanio is excited when speaking about Portia and uses strong classical imagery to describe her.
• Shylock repeats the same phrase, showing he is preoccupied with the idea of revenge.

The Elizabethans were quite familiar with the language of courtly love.

• All the lovers get carried away when describing their partners. They use the language of love poetry, showing the intensity of their feelings. Sometimes they try too hard.
• Lancelot tries to use clever words, but fails. This shows that he would like to climb up the social ladder but is unlikely to be able to.

PART FOUR

STUDY SKILLS

HOW TO USE QUOTATIONS

One of the secrets of success in writing essays is the way you use quotations. There are five basic principles:

- Put inverted commas at the beginning and end of the quotation
- Write the quotation exactly as it appears in the original
- Do not use a quotation that repeats what you have just written
- Use the quotation so that it fits into your sentence
- Keep the quotation as short as possible

Quotations should be used to develop the line of thought in your essays.

Your comments should not duplicate what is in the quotation. For example:

> Shylock warns us that he is as fierce as a dog: 'since I am a dog beware my fangs'.

Far more effective is to write:

> Shylock's revenge springs from his inhuman treatment by Christians: 'Since I am a dog beware my fangs'.

Always lay out the lines as they appear in the text. For example:

> Bassanio encourages Gratiano to have some fun at the party,
> '... for we have friends
> That purpose merriment.'

or

> Bassanio encourages Gratiano to have some fun at the party,
> '...for we have friends/That purpose merriment.'

However, the most sophisticated way of using the writer's words is to embed them into your sentence:

> Shylock warns those who have treated him as 'a dog' to 'beware my fangs'.

When you use quotations in this way, you are demonstrating the ability to use text as evidence to support your ideas - not simply including words from the original to prove you have read it.

Everyone writes differently. Work through the suggestions given here and adapt the advice to suit your own style and interests. This will improve your essay-writing skills and allow your personal voice to emerge.

The following points indicate in ascending order the skills of essay writing:

- Picking out one or two facts about the story and adding the odd detail
- Writing about the text by retelling the story
- Retelling the story and adding a quotation here and there
- Organising an answer which explains what is happening in the text and giving quotations to support what you write

....

- Writing in such a way as to show that you have thought about the intentions of the writer of the text and that you understand the techniques used
- Writing at some length, giving your viewpoint on the text and commenting by picking out details to support your views
- Looking at the text as a work of art, demonstrating clear critical judgement and explaining to the reader of your essay how the enjoyment of the text is assisted by literary devices, linguistic effects and psychological insights; showing how the text relates to the time when it was written

The dotted line above represents the division between lower- and higher-level grades. Higher-level performance begins when you start to consider your response as a reader of the text. The highest level is reached when you offer an enthusiastic personal response and show how this piece of literature is a product of its time.

Coursework   Set aside an hour or so at the start of your work and
essay   plan what you have to do.

- List all the points you feel are needed to cover the task. Collect page references of information and quotations that will support what you have to say. A helpful tool is the highlighter pen: this saves painstaking copying and enables you to target precisely what you want to use.
- Focus on what you consider to be the main points of the essay. Try to sum up your argument in a single sentence, which could be the closing sentence of your essay. Depending on the essay title, it could be a statement about a character: Portia is the wittiest character in the play. She is very good at playing word games with Bassanio and Nerissa and it is Portia who outwits Shylock when all other attempts have failed; an opinion about a setting: I believe that Shylock is a product of the environment in which he has lived. He has been made cruel by years of ill treatment; or a judgement on a theme: I think the main theme of the play is that life is full of trials. Some are trials of loyalty, others are tests to see whether someone can tell right from wrong.
- Make a short essay plan. Use the first paragraph to introduce the argument you wish to make. In the following paragraphs develop this argument with details, examples and other possible points of view. Sum up your argument in the last paragraph. Check you have answered the question.
- Write the essay, remembering all the time the central point you are making.
- On completion, go back over what you have written to eliminate careless errors and improve expression. Read it aloud to yourself, or, if you are feeling more confident, to a relative or friend.

If you can, try to type your essay using a word

processor. This will allow you to correct and improve your writing without spoiling its appearance.

Examination
essay

The essay written in an examination often carries more marks than the coursework essay even though it is written under considerable time pressure.

In the revision period build up notes on various aspects of the text you are using. Fortunately, in acquiring this set of York Notes on *The Merchant of Venice*, you have made a prudent beginning! York Notes are set out to give you vital information and help you to construct your personal overview of the text.

Make notes with appropriate quotations about the key issues of the set text. Go into the examination knowing your text and having a clear set of opinions about it.

In the
examination

In most English Literature examinations you can take in copies of your set books. This is an enormous advantage although it may lull you into a false sense of security. Beware! There is simply not enough time in an examination to read the book from scratch.

- Read the question paper carefully and remind yourself what you have to do.
- Look at the questions on your set texts to select the one that most interests you and mentally work out the points you wish to stress.
- Remind yourself of the time available and how you are going to use it.
- Briefly map out a short plan in note form that will keep your writing on track and illustrate the key argument you want to make.
- Then set about writing it.
- When you have finished, check through to eliminate errors.

To summarise,
these are keys
to success

- **Know the play**
- **Have a clear understanding of and opinions on the storyline, characters, setting, themes and writer's concerns**

• Select the right material
• Plan and write a clear response, continually bearing the question in mind

SAMPLE ESSAY PLAN

A typical essay question on *The Merchant of Venice* is followed by a sample essay plan in note form. This does not present the only answer to the question, merely one. Do not be afraid to include your own ideas, and leave out some of those in the sample!

How much do you think Shylock has been influenced by the environment in which he lives?

The essay needs an introduction, main argument and a conclusion.

Introduction   Shylock is useful to the Christians only because he does something which they are not allowed to do.

Part 1   Explain what his particular environment is; the points below develop this idea:
• Act I, Scene 3, Bassanio is effectively going to his local bank to ask for a loan, yet he is not always polite.
• Antonio kicks and spits at Shylock simply because he does not like the way the moneylender does business – quote examples of Antonio's behaviour.
• Act II, Scene 2, Lancelot, Shylock's servant gives a disrespectful opinion of his master. His words are full of anti-Semitic remarks and some of his jokes are in poor taste.
• Act III, Scene 1, Salarino and Solanio continue the victimisation of Shylock, even though they know he is upset at his daughter's disappearance.
This establishes the type of behaviour that Shylock had to put up with. Mention the law always being on the side of the Christians, and Jews having to wear special clothes to make them stand out.

Part 2

The next stage is to look at the type of man he is:
- when going about his own business
- when confronted by the Christians

The two scenes with Tubal show Shylock with a fellow Jew. Look at how Tubal regards Shylock, e.g. Act III, Scene 1, Tubal is not particularly sympathetic towards Shylock. Tubal probably suffers the same treatment as Shylock yet he seems less bitter.
- Shylock does not have a very close relationship with Jessica
- He wants to see his daughter punished rather than wanting to forgive her

When confronted by the Christians, Shylock fights his corner:
- He tricks Antonio into swearing to the bond
- He is delighted to hear that Antonio's ships have been lost
- He takes great delight in taunting Gratiano, Bassanio and Antonio
- He goes too far in his search for revenge
- He is foolish enough to try to use the Christian laws against a Christian
- He is severely punished for his attempt on Antonio's life

His big mistake is to think that the law can be used for his benefit.

Conclusion

No definite answer
- Shylock has been more strongly affected by his treatment than other Jews have
- He is partly the product of his environment but some of his behaviour is because of his own character
- His character has been formed whilst living in this society and so the harsh treatment he receives is responsible for a large degree of his hatred.

1 By examining his treatment of Portia and Shylock, discuss the idea that Shakespeare was neither racist nor sexist.

2 People tend to be shaped by the environment in which they live. By exploring the behaviour of any two characters from *The Merchant of Venice*, say how true you think this is.

3 The play is full of trials. Say what any two of the following reveal about the characters involved:
a The test of the caskets
b Shylock and Antonio in court
c The test of the rings

4 The play deals with different ideas of right and wrong. Examine the feelings and actions of two of the following characters and say what each one feels about this idea:
a Shylock
b Portia
c Antonio
d Jessica

5 Discuss the way in which Shakespeare explores the different kinds of bonds which exist between people. You should consider:
a The bond of friendship
b The bond of marriage
c Bonds made in business

6 'Belmont is a woman's world, whilst Venice is a man's' – consider this quotation.

7 What do you learn about the Elizabethan view of the world from the attitudes shown in the play?

8 Discuss the difficulties and advantages of staging the play today.

PART FIVE

CULTURAL CONNECTIONS

BROADER PERSPECTIVES

Plays and films

The Merchant of Venice was written and first performed in the England of the late sixteenth century, yet it remains one of the most frequently performed plays today. Its themes of friendship, betrayal and religious intolerance are as relevant in the twentieth century as they were in Shakespeare's time.

Many recent productions have focused upon the treatment of the Jews in Nazi Germany and have used ideas from this period of history. The Royal Shakespeare Company's 1987 production with Antony Sher as Shylock featured swastikas and anti-Semitic propaganda scrawled on the walls of Venice. The Oscar-winning Spielberg film *Schindler's List* gives an account of Jewish persecution under the Nazis and contains similar ideas at times to those in the play.

The existence of Apartheid in South Africa and the Man Act in the southern United States of America were recent reminders that behaviour like that of Antonio does not go away, it simply changes where it operates. Four hundred years after the play was written, someone, somewhere will behave like the characters in *The Merchant of Venice*.

A modern audience cannot look at the play without feeling uncomfortable at some of the lines. Rather than being a hindrance, this is one of the very reasons that *The Merchant of Venice* is still so popular. It makes the audience of today look at intolerance and draw its own conclusions as to whether it is acceptable or not.

The following sources might be helpful to you:

Books

Schindler's Ark by Thomas Keneally (1983), on which the film *Schindler's List* was based, tells the

Y

story of a man who helped Jews to escape from the Nazis.

To Kill a Mockingbird by Harper Lee (1966) deals with racial prejudice in the southern United States.

Roll of Thunder Hear My Cry by Mildred Taylor (1976, Penguin 1997) follows a similar theme to *Mockingbird*.

bathos movement from a very important subject to a trivial one. The result is often a ludicrous comparison

blank verse lines which have rhythm, but do not rhyme. Most of the play is in blank verse, with *iambic pentameter* as the type of verse used

confidant(e) a friend of the chief character whom he/she entrusts with information, providing a useful method of letting the audience know his/her motives

heroic couplet two rhyming lines of *iambic pentameter*. Shakespeare often uses an heroic couplet to signify the end of a scene or to announce something very important

iambic pentameter a line of poetry with five pairs of syllables arranged in the following order: unstressed then stressed. Most of the speeches in the play are in *iambic pentameter* e.g. 'But còme, I'll tèll thee àll my whòle de-vìce'

malapropism using the wrong word without realising it. The word "malapropism" comes from the character Mrs Malaprop in Sheridan's play *The Rivals*. She continually tried to impress by using long words, but ended

up speaking nonsense. This was known in Shakespeare's day as 'cacozelia'

metre another word for rhythm. There are many different types of rhythm. Each different type is simply a different arrangement of stressed and unstressed syllables

pathos a quality which evokes feelings of pity and sorrow in the audience

patronage the support by a wealthy person for an artist, writer etc. For many years artists of all kinds had to rely upon patrons for financial support; this probably includes Shakespeare

prose what we would call 'ordinary speech', prose has no set pattern of rhythm

pun a play on words. The Elizabethans were very fond of puns and they considered that someone who could pun well was intelligent. Sometimes this can go too far, as Lorenzo points out to Lancelot, and is used for comic effect when a character puns at every opportunity

rhyming couplet adjacent lines of any verse form which rhyme

tragicomedy a mixture of tragedy and comedy. *The Merchant of Venice* is a tragicomedy as the play does not have the tragic ending that it could

y

TEST YOURSELF (Act I)

A 1 Antonio *(1.42)*
∴ 2 Bassanio *(1.114)*
   3 Antonio *(3.172)*
   4 Portia *(2.97)*
   5 Shylock *(3.34)*
   6 Antonio *(3.55)*
   7 Antonio *(3.98–9)*
   8 Antonio *(1.145)*
   9 Antonio *(1.138)*

TEST YOURSELF (Act II)

A 1 Portia *(1.15–16)*
∴ 2 Lancelot *(2.86)*
   3 Jessica *(3.16)*
   4 Shylock *(5.44)*
   5 Solanio *(8.15–16)*
   6 Lorenzo *(6.36–7)*
   7 To Nerissa, about Morocco *(7.79)*
   8 Portia *(9.100)*

TEST YOURSELF (Act III)

A 1 Portia *(2.16)*
∴ 2 Bassanio *(2.183–4)*
   3 Jessica *(2.289)*
   4 Antonio *(3.26)*
   5 Lancelot *(5.12)*

   6 Lorenzo *(5.72–3)*
   7 Antonio *(2.260)*
   8 Antonio *(3.6)*
   9 Shylock *(2.298)*

TEST YOURSELF (Act IV)

A 1 The Duke *(1.3–4)*
∴ 2 Shylock *(1.59)*
   3 Bassanio *(1.112–13)*
   4 Gratiano *(1.128–9)*
   5 Portia *(1.180–9)*
   6 Shylock *(1.221)*
   7 Portia *(1.232)*
   8 Shylock *(1.319)*
   9 Shylock *(1.343)*

TEST YOURSELF (Act V)

A 1 Lorenzo *(1.1)*
∴ 2 Jessica *(1.23)*
   3 Lancelot *(1.47)*
   4 Portia *(1.91)*
   5 Portia *(1.137)*
   6 Gratiano *(1.144)*
   7 Lorenzo *(1.30–1)*
   8 Lancelot *(1.43)*
   9 Nerissa *(1.93)*
   10 Portia *(1.248)*

Notes

York Notes Advanced (£3.99 each)

Margaret Atwood
The Handmaid's Tale

Jane Austen
Emma

Jane Austen
Pride and Prejudice

William Blake
Songs of Innocence and of Experience

Charlotte Brontë
Jane Eyre

Emily Brontë
Wuthering Heights

Geoffrey Chaucer
*The Wife of Bath's Prologue
and Tale*

Joseph Conrad
Heart of Darkness

Charles Dickens
Great Expectations

F. Scott Fitzgerald
The Great Gatsby

Thomas Hardy
Tess of the d'Urbervilles

Seamus Heaney
Selected Poems

James Joyce
Dubliners

Arthur Miller
Death of a Salesman

William Shakespeare
Antony and Cleopatra

William Shakespeare
Hamlet

William Shakespeare
King Lear

William Shakespeare
The Merchant of Venice

William Shakespeare
Much Ado About Nothing

William Shakespeare
Othello

William Shakespeare
Romeo and Juliet

William Shakespeare
The Tempest

Mary Shelley
Frankenstein

Alice Walker
The Color Purple

Tennessee Williams
A Streetcar Named Desire

John Webster
The Duchess of Malfi

GCSE and equivalent levels (£3.50 each)

Harold Brighouse
Hobson's Choice

Charles Dickens
Great Expectations

Charles Dickens
Hard Times

George Eliot
Silas Marner

William Golding
Lord of the Flies

Thomas Hardy
The Mayor of Casterbridge

Susan Hill
I'm the King of the Castle

Barry Hines
A Kestrel for a Knave

Harper Lee
To Kill a Mockingbird

Arthur Miller
A View from the Bridge

Arthur Miller
The Crucible

George Orwell
Animal Farm

J.B. Priestley
An Inspector Calls

J.D. Salinger
The Catcher in the Rye

William Shakespeare
Macbeth

William Shakespeare
The Merchant of Venice

William Shakespeare
Romeo and Juliet

William Shakespeare
Twelfth Night

George Bernard Shaw
Pygmalion

John Steinbeck
Of Mice and Men

Mildred D. Taylor
Roll of Thunder, Hear My Cry

James Watson
Talking in Whispers

A Choice of Poets

Nineteenth Century Short Stories

Poetry of the First World War

Chinua Achebe
Things Fall Apart

Edward Albee
Who's Afraid of Virginia Woolf?

Jane Austen
Mansfield Park

Jane Austen
Northanger Abbey

Jane Austen
Persuasion

Jane Austen
Sense and Sensibility

Samuel Beckett
Waiting for Godot

Alan Bennett
Talking Heads

John Betjeman
Selected Poems

Robert Bolt
A Man for All Seasons

Robert Burns
Selected Poems

Lord Byron
Selected Poems

Geoffrey Chaucer
The Franklin's Tale

Geoffrey Chaucer
The Merchant's Tale

Geoffrey Chaucer
The Miller's Tale

Geoffrey Chaucer
The Nun's Priest's Tale

Geoffrey Chaucer
Prologue to the Canterbury Tales

Samuel Taylor Coleridge
Selected Poems

Daniel Defoe
Moll Flanders

Daniel Defoe
Robinson Crusoe

Shelagh Delaney
A Taste of Honey

Charles Dickens
Bleak House

Charles Dickens
Oliver Twist

Emily Dickinson
Selected Poems

John Donne
Selected Poems

Douglas Dunn
Selected Poems

George Eliot
Middlemarch

George Eliot
The Mill on the Floss

T.S. Eliot
The Waste Land

T.S. Eliot
Selected Poems

Henry Fielding
Joseph Andrews

E.M. Forster
Howards End

E.M. Forster
A Passage to India

John Fowles
The French Lieutenant's Woman

Brian Friel
Translations

Elizabeth Gaskell
North and South

Oliver Goldsmith
She Stoops to Conquer

Graham Greene
Brighton Rock

Thomas Hardy
Jude the Obscure

Thomas Hardy
Selected Poems

Nathaniel Hawthorne
The Scarlet Letter

Ernest Hemingway
The Old Man and the Sea

Homer
The Iliad

Homer
The Odyssey

Aldous Huxley
Brave New World

Ben Jonson
The Alchemist

Ben Jonson
Volpone

James Joyce
A Portrait of the Artist as a Young Man

John Keats
Selected Poems

Philip Larkin
Selected Poems

D.H. Lawrence
The Rainbow

D.H. Lawrence
Sons and Lovers

D.H. Lawrence
Women in Love

Christopher Marlowe
Doctor Faustus

John Milton
Paradise Lost Bks I & II

John Milton
Paradise Lost IV & IX

Sean O'Casey
Juno and the Paycock

George Orwell
Nineteen Eighty-four

John Osborne
Look Back in Anger

Wilfred Owen
Selected Poems

Harold Pinter
The Caretaker

Sylvia Plath
Selected Works

Alexander Pope
Selected Poems

Jean Rhys
Wide Sargasso Sea

William Shakespeare
As You Like It

William Shakespeare
Coriolanus

William Shakespeare
Henry IV Pt 1

William Shakespeare
Henry V

William Shakespeare
Julius Caesar

William Shakespeare
Measure for Measure

William Shakespeare
Much Ado About Nothing

William Shakespeare
A Midsummer Night's Dream

William Shakespeare
Richard II

William Shakespeare
Richard III

William Shakespeare
Sonnets

William Shakespeare
The Taming of the Shrew

William Shakespeare
The Winter's Tale

George Bernard Shaw
Arms and the Man

George Bernard Shaw
Saint Joan

Richard Brinsley Sheridan
The Rivals

Muriel Spark
The Prime of Miss Jean Brodie

John Steinbeck
The Grapes of Wrath

John Steinbeck
The Pearl

Tom Stoppard
Rosencrantz and Guildenstern are Dead

Jonathan Swift
Gulliver's Travels

John Millington Synge
The Playboy of the Western World

W.M. Thackeray
Vanity Fair

Virgil
The Aeneid

Derek Walcott
Selected Poems

Oscar Wilde
The Importance of Being Earnest

Tennessee Williams
Cat on a Hot Tin Roof

Tennessee Williams
The Glass Menagerie

Virginia Woolf
Mrs Dalloway

Virginia Woolf
To the Lighthouse

William Wordsworth
Selected Poems

W.B. Yeats
Selected Poems

York Notes – the Ultimate Literature Guides

York Notes are recognised as the best literature study guides.
If you have enjoyed using this book and have found it useful, you
can now order others directly from us – simply follow the ordering
instructions below.

HOW TO ORDER

Decide which title(s) you require and then order in one of the following
ways:

Booksellers
All titles available from good bookstores.

By post
List the title(s) you require in the space provided overleaf,
select your method of payment, complete your name and
address details and return your completed order form and
payment to:
Addison Wesley Longman Ltd
PO BOX 88
Harlow
Essex CM19 5SR

By phone
Call our Customer Information Centre on 01279 623923 to
place your order, quoting mail number: HEYN1.

By fax
Complete the order form overleaf, ensuring you fill in your
name and address details and method of payment, and fax it
to us on 01279 414130.

By e-mail
E-mail your order to us on awlhe.orders@awl.co.uk listing
title(s) and quantity required and providing full name and
address details as requested overleaf. Please quote mail
number: HEYN1. Please do not send credit card details by
e-mail.

York Notes Order Form

Titles required:

Quantity	Title/ISBN	Price

Sub total _____

Please add £2.50 postage & packing _____

(P & P is free for orders over £50) _____

Total _____

Mail no: HEYN1

Your Name _____

Your Address _____

_____

Postcode _____ Telephone _____

Method of payment

☐ I enclose a cheque or a P/O for £_____ made payable to Addison Wesley Longman Ltd

☐ Please charge my Visa/Access/AMEX/Diners Club card

Number _____ Expiry Date _____

Signature _____ Date _____

(please ensure that the address given above is the same as for your credit card)

Prices and other details are correct at time of going to press but may change without notice. All orders are subject to status.

☐ *Please tick this box if you would like a complete listing of Longman Study Guides (suitable for GCSE and A-level students)*

York Press

Longman

Addison
Wesley
Longman